spiritual encou

Waiti
on *the Lord*

STEPHEN D & JACALYN EYRE

SCRIPTURE UNION

SCRIPTURE UNION
207-209 Queensway, Bletchley, Milton Keynes, MK2 2EB, England

First published in the United States by InterVarsity Press

First published in Great Britain by Scripture Union, 1995

Unless otherwise indicated, Scripture quotations are taken from the HOLY BIBLE, NEW INTERNATIONAL VERSION. Copyright © 1973, 1978, 1984 by International Bible Society. Anglicisation copyright © 1979, 1984, 1989. Used by permission of Hodder and Stoughton Limited.

Cover illustration: Brady Senior
Cover design: Mark Carpenter Design Consultants

ISBN 1 85999 019 3

Printed in England by Stanley L Hunt (Printers) Ltd, Midland Road, Rushden, Northants

Introducing *Waiting on the Lord*

I hate to wait.

If I (Steve) have to stand in line at a fast food restaurant for more than a couple of minutes, I become impatient. I arrange to arrive at an airport as close to departure time as possible. If I have any time to spare at the gate, I look for a phone to make a few calls or at least pull out a book to read. I hate to wait in traffic behind a line of backed-up cars. I don't like to wait for my family to get ready to go somewhere. I don't like waiting in line at the post office. It's not that I am impatient, you understand. At least that is what I tell myself. It's just that I don't like to waste time.

My life with God has been a continual battle over the issue of waiting. When I say go, God frequently says stop. When I say now, God frequently says later. As God challenges me, I find that my impatience with waiting is really an issue of control. When I have to wait, someone else has taken charge of my time. If I have to wait in line at McDonald's, then I can't get on to my next project. If I have to wait at the airport, then I can't be in my office getting my work done. If I have to wait in traffic, then I can't get to my destination when I want to.

God's school of spiritual maturity for me has included a major emphasis on waiting. Sometimes that waiting required long delayed answers to prayer. Sometimes the waiting required ministry with little evidence of fruit. Sometimes it required putting aside cherished plans for a long time.

Waiting for God is required because, as my Lord, he is in charge of my life. Experiencing God's discipline of waiting, I am taken deeper into the knowledge of God and myself. Richard Hendrix writes, "Second only to suffering, waiting may be the greatest teacher and trainer in godliness, maturity and genuine spirituality most of us ever encounter."

I don't believe that my experience with God is unusual. It is the way of God to require us to wait on him. Abraham had to wait twenty-five years for Isaac. During that time he became God's intimate friend and through him the bloodline of Israel and the Messiah was established. Moses had to wait forty years in the desert for the Promised Land. During that time he wrote the law and was invited into intimacy with God. Through his work, Israel was transformed from a collection of slaves into an organized nation. David had to wait ten years in the desert before he ascended the throne. During that time he learned to govern by leading the fugitives who joined him.

We must learn to wait on the Lord, not because there is time to waste but because it is the most efficient and effective way to get things, the most important things, done. Some time ago Bill Hybels wrote a book called *Too Busy Not to Pray*. Good title and a good book too. Prayer and waiting are intimately connected. In the kingdom of God we can also say that we are *too busy not to wait*.

The Benefits of Waiting

There are different kinds of waiting. There is the eager yet laborious waiting of a mother expecting the birth of her child, the busy waiting of a college student to get through the senior year and get into the "real" world. There is the passive waiting of a traveler in a terminal anticipating her plane to arrive. There is also the troubled waiting of a patient anticipating a call for test results from his doctor. And then there is waiting on the Lord. Waiting on the Lord combines all the preceding types of waiting with a rich variety of spiritual dynamics.

Waiting on the Lord means living in a supernatural world. We come to know that the outcome of our personal efforts is guided by the Person who is the shaping hand of all events—past, present and future.

Waiting on God unleashes spiritual power. When we wait on God, he comes to us with resources beyond what we naturally have. As Isaiah wrote, "They that wait upon the LORD shall renew their strength; they shall mount up with wings as eagles; they shall run, and not be weary;

and they shall walk, and not faint" (40:31).

Waiting on the Lord brings you into divine-human partnership. God works through people to bring his kingdom and achieve his purposes. God and Abraham, God and Noah, God and Moses, God and Paul are just a few of the divine-human partnerships that have shaped history. Just as a marriage consists of a partnership between a man and a woman, so life requires the partnership of human and Creator.

Waiting on the Lord means developing your potential. By waiting, our gifts, talents, abilities and character are focused and fulfilled. God works with us and through us as we depend on him.

Waiting on the Lord does not mean passiveness. It means learning to act in dependence on our Creator by drawing on his divine resources.

Waiting on the Lord means living with an eager sense of anticipation. Because we can't truly achieve without God carrying out his end of the partnership, we work and live with hope for what he will do.

Waiting on the Lord means being able to cope with a sense of desperation. God has been described as an "eleventh-hour God." When things get down to the wire, we will find ourselves longing for God to work, with the sure knowledge that he will.

Learning to Wait on the Lord
The textbook for waiting on the Lord is the Psalms. This is not just because there you frequently run into phrases like "How long Lord?" "Come quickly to help me," and "I wait for you, Lord." It is because throughout the Psalms you find a tone of dependence and anticipation. Those who wrote the Psalms knew that life was meant to be lived in partnership of the human and the divine.

The Psalms record both the experiences and the inner lives of world-class waiters. Through the medium of Hebrew poetry, we discover that waiting in the Lord is a life of adventure, danger, exaltation and desperation. In one psalm David is boasting in the Lord, in the next he is seething at his enemies and in the next he is in the depths of despair. Through the experiences and emotions recorded by David and the rest of the psalmists, we are challenged and released to feel and experience the presence of God. Three years of seminary taught me to think about God; meditating in the Psalms taught me to think *and* feel with God.

You will work through Psalms 30—40. Why these psalms? Because

they are cherished "friends." We clung to these particular psalms when
Steve was in the midst of a career change and an identity crisis and our
family was living crossculturally. During that time, from these psalms we
found encouragement to wait with confidence for the next phase of life.

The quiet times are arranged in cycles of two to five on each chapter.
Each day we ask you to read the whole chapter and then focus in on the
verses for that particular day. This will help you begin to experience the
rhythms of the psalmist.

Writing this guide was a team effort. In the introductions you'll read
stories from Steve's experience, and in the study sections you'll see more
of Jackie's hand.

Guided Quiet Times

You can't just read the Psalms casually and expect to get out of them
what the author intends. Like all poetry, they were written to be pon-
dered, savored and experienced. We seek to help you learn from the
Psalms through the use of several spiritual disciplines. We will lead you
in the use of inductive Bible study, settling exercises, silence and soli-
tude, prayer, and the meditative tools of picturing and reflecting.

Some people think of a quiet time as Bible study and prayer. We think
of a quiet time as an encounter with God in which you do Bible study
and pray. The difference between the two definitions may seem small,
but we think it is crucial. If a quiet time is just Bible study and prayer,
then the relational dimension may easily get lost. You may end up
merely going through the motions of religious activities and gaining
some new information. However, if your goal is to set aside time to meet
with God, then the whole dynamic of the quiet time is changed. It
becomes a cultivation of a relationship. It becomes an opportunity for
discipleship as the Lord himself meets with us.

Of course, because God's Word is his means of instructing us, we can't
expect to learn from him unless we are spending serious time considering what has been written down for us. Likewise, prayer is the means
by which we talk with him and ask for his help. But we must be careful
that prayer involves listening as well as asking. If we allow our prayer
to degenerate into offering God a list of our wants and recommendations
for running the world, then we are no longer in a personal teacher-stu-
dent relationship.

The format for each day includes five elements.

Introduction: This is brief, a couple of paragraphs that allow us to set the tone and introduce the issues for your quiet time.

Approach: This is designed to help you deal with mental and emotional obstacles that we all struggle with as we seek to shift our attention from ourselves to God and his Word. Take some time with the approach question, five minutes or more. Use it to reach out to God so that you know you are meeting with him as you begin your study of his Word.

Study: These questions are written to help you focus on the content of the passage. The questions focus on the essential issues of each passage and on what they mean.

The New International Version is the translation we used to write the Spiritual Encounter Guide study questions. You can use another version, of course, but you will need to make adjustments as some of the questions may not make sense. Why the NIV? We think it is a good contemporary translation that brings out the meaning of the original texts.

Reflect: In this section, we use the spiritual tools of silence and imagination to help you apply the passage to your soul and life issues. As with the approach question, the more time you take with these questions, the more likely you will be to come away from your quiet time with a sense of personal encounter.

Pray: We offer a couple of suggestions for prayer. We expect that during this time you will develop your own prayer list as well. Take time to ask God for help and wisdom for yourself, your family, church, friends and whatever else you can think of.

Each quiet time will take you a minimum of twenty to thirty minutes, although you could easily spend more time if you work through the questions in a leisurely, reflective manner.

With Hopeful Anticipation
Working through these psalms will alter the way you experience life. God will become more present to you in everything that you do. You may find you feel pain more deeply and joy more intensely. We hope you find your heart slipping into the quiet gratitude of a life filled with waiting for your Lord.

DAY 1

Satisfied Anticipation
Psalm 30:1-5

M ajor corporations are laying off large numbers of workers in the latest rage of downsizing. Those who have gotten a pink slip do their best to cover it, but you can see the pain in their eyes. Even those who have a job now don't know if they will next year. There is a sword of uncertainty that hangs over us. Major purchases are put on hold and vacation plans are scrapped. Our programs and plans for ministry at the church are put on hold as well, because people who aren't working or who fear they may lose their jobs find tithing difficult.

One of our basic human needs is security. We work hard to establish a career for job security. We also seek to accumulate money in the bank in pursuit of financial security. Relational security is important too. If we feel insecure or threatened by someone else, our emotions and thoughts become preoccupied with ways to defend ourselves.

In the end, if our security, in any area, is dependent upon our own resources and abilities, then we must live in constant vigilance. How much better if the Creator of the universe were in charge of protecting us! In this psalm David relates the experience of looking to God for his security. He found it both a humbling and a thrilling experience.

Approach: Settling in God's Presence

As soon as our family gets into the car, there is a debate about who gets to choose the music on the radio. When our sons have their turn, the music is always driving and loud. We do our best to talk through the music. However, eventually, despite the protests, we turn it down. And after a while, if the conversation requires it, we say, "That's it for today; we need to talk." We need to do the same thing if we are to have a serious conversation with God. Imagine that you have turned off the radio that was blaring away inside you. Sit for a while in the quiet. You may find that there are internal protests as you seek to get quiet. Write down your thoughts and impressions.

Study

1. Read all of Psalm 30. No one knows for sure what the problem was, but from the words *depths, healed, enemies, grave* and *pit,* what dangers might David have been facing?

2. Read the whole psalm again. List the range of emotions that are described.

Place the emotions on the range of painful to pleasurable.

Painful   Pleasurable

3. David acknowledges that both pain and pleasure come from God. To paraphrase David in verse 5:

God's anger leads to weeping,
   God's favor causes rejoicing.
God's anger doesn't last,
   but his favor does.
God's anger feels like the dark of night,
   God's favor like the bright rising sun.

What insight into life does David gain by acknowledging that painful as well as pleasurable experiences come from God?

What insight about God does David gain by acknowledging that God is occasionally angry with him?

Reflect
1. Consider a dark time in your life. What was going on?

What range of feelings did you experience?

What did you learn about God?

What did you learn about yourself?

How has it affected you?

2. David's response to God covers a wide range of emotions. Examine your own emotional responses to God during the past month or so. Where on the line below would you place your mark?

_____

Apathetic   Angry   Grateful   Exulting

Pray
Give thanks to God for the ways he has been a help to you in the hard places of your life.

Ask God to help you face the pressures of life that you are now under.

Ask God to make your church a place where people can worship and exalt God in heart and voice.

DAY 2

Security in the Lord
Psalm 30:6-12

*O*ccasionally I experience what I call the "jerked rug" phenomenon. It seems to come when I am feeling pretty good about myself, a bit too good. When the rug gets pulled and I stumble, I find that I am not quite as clever as I thought or as wise as I wanted to believe.

Over the years I have come to appreciate these experiences as gifts of God. If he allowed me to continue in my own self-generating confidence, pride would become a hardened shell around my heart. But when the pressures of life become greater than I can handle, I am forced to face my own limitations. It is during those times that I experience anew the wonderful grace of a God who is there to give security far beyond my own capacity.

Approach: Settling in God's Presence
Ever have a closet so full of clutter that you were afraid to open it? Often

our hearts are like closets into which we throw unwanted feelings and unsatisfied desires. After a while, we don't want to open the door because all those unpleasant things will fall out and make a mess. The problem is that if our hearts are cluttered, the spiritual and emotional dimension of life is lost. Take some time now to open up your heart. Allow things to fall out. Over the course of this study you will be asking God to help you clean it up. Write down what desires, hurts and concerns you find. After you have done that, sit in quiet anticipation of what God will do.

Study

1. Read Psalm 30. How do verses 6 and 7 describe David's sense of dependence on God?

2. What reasons does David present to God in favor of his deliverance (vv. 9-10)?

3. In what different ways does David express exultation for his deliverance (vv. 11-12)?

4. Look over the entire psalm. How would you describe David's relationship with God?

5. Waiting on the Lord doesn't have to be passive. How is David actively waiting throughout this psalm?

Reflect

1. Difficult circumstances can cause us to reflect on the character of God. How have the circumstances of your life affected your relationship with God?

2. David expresses some of the ups and downs of his life. Consider the last six months to a year of your life and then chart your ups and downs.

	1	2	3	4	5	6
Highs						
Lows						

3. Meditate through the ups and downs, picturing the Lord with you through each phase. Once you have done that, write down your insights and emotions.

Pray

Ask God to give you the courage to face the unpleasant experiences of life that may be unresolved.

Ask God to give the members of your church the courage to face unpleasant conflicts that are important but unresolved.

Ask God to bring the nations to face the unpleasant experiences of life that are producing conflict.

DAY 3
Rescued from Idolaters
Psalm 31:1-8

We live in a turbulent time. *Culture Wars* is a very fitting title for one book that describes the increasing conflict of values we are experiencing as we move into a post-Christian society. There are now many different belief systems, both secular and religious, which are competing for our allegiance.

While the turbulence created by these clashing belief systems seems new, the clash has been going on in different forms for thousands of years. In this psalm David affirms his choice to trust in the Lord rather than in the popular idols of his age. In the current culture war, we need to do the same.

As you make the choice for God, do it with your eyes open. Commitment to God as the one true God is bound to make Christians unpopular. You may find yourself accused of prejudice and bigotry. It is possible that as the culture war heats up, your faith may cost you in the near future —perhaps a promotion, your job or even friends and family members.

How should Christians respond? Considerable material is being written on this, with more to come. There is one thing I am convinced of: cultural conflict should not lead us on a new crusade to punish and destroy the heretics and infidels. Nor should it lead us into defensive huddles of "true believers." We need to look at the example of David, who took his licks while trusting God for his protection.

Approach: Settling in God's Presence
On my desk there is a little sign given to me by my small group. It says, "Be still and know that I am God." It's very appropriate. I always feel as if there is more to do than there is time to do it. And frequently, when I am in one place, I find that I am already thinking about the next place that I have to be. This sense of drivenness leads to an abundance of experiences half enjoyed and superficially considered. One of the ways I combat this drivenness is to write down everything I have to do. Then in a time of silent reflection, I give the list over to God and ask him to be responsible for it. When I do that, I find there is a deep and quiet peace inside.

As you begin your quiet time, make a list of everything you have to do and give it over to God. If God blesses you with a sense of peace, just sit for a while and enjoy his presence before you move on to study.

Study
1. Read Psalm 31. After you have read it, focus on verses 1-8. This is a psalm of urgency. What does David want from God?

2. David feels threatened. What words does he use to describe his plight?

3. What words and images does David use for God?

Describe in your own words how David is thinking about God.

4. What does David know about God that gives him the desire to wait for God's help?

Reflect
1. David's first request is to be delivered from shame (v. 1). Reflect back on your life: When have you experienced situations that caused you shame?

How did it affect you?

2. Imagine God surrounding you like a fortress and supporting you like a large rock. After resting in the security of God's protection, write down your thoughts and emotions.

3. When have you felt a sense of urgency and had to wait for God to act?

What was the outcome of your experience of waiting?

Pray
Ask God to protect you from humiliating situations.

Ask God to make your family a place where people feel his protection and support.

Pray that your church may be a community of people who protect each other rather than criticize each other.

DAY 4
Rejection and Danger
Psalm 31:9-18

*A*s a Christian leader, I spend my professional life in front of people. My thoughts, plans and actions have effects on others. This of course brings occasion not only for favorable comment, of which I have had my share. It also brings occasion for unfavorable comment, of which I also have had my share. It's during the times of unfavorable comment that I find Christian ministry the hardest. These times bring an uncomfortable sense of isolation.

Whether you are in a position of public responsibility or not, you too have experienced times when it seems that fellow students, neighbors or colleagues are talking about you. Not infrequently there may be a person or two who are glad for your disfavor and who do what they can to feed the flames.

How do we as Christians respond during such uncomfortable times? Surprisingly, we are not called to the way of emotional denial and a stiff upper lip. David shows us a way that allows us to be both free to hurt and free to call out to God for comfort and help.

Approach: Settling in God's Presence

Conversations are enjoyable. Monologues are boring. I believe that this is one of the reasons many find prayer difficult. We feel as if we are supposed to talk *at* God for five or ten minutes. The pressure to keep up the flow of words is draining.

Instead of approaching God with a flow of words, approach him with silence today. Just sit quietly for several minutes. Relax in God's presence and enjoy the peace of being with someone you trust so much that you don't have to say anything. If prayer concerns come up, write them down. At the end of your quiet time, come back to these concerns and ask God to deal with them.

Study

1. Read Psalm 31. One of the reasons that we find the psalms helpful is the intensity of emotions expressed and the rich variety of descriptive words used. What graphic words does David use in verses 9-13 to describe his plight?

2. What words and ideas in verses 9-13 convey David's sense of isolation?

3. What are several of the things David wants from God, according to verses 14-18?

4. How does the phrase "my times are in your hands" summarize his sense of waiting on God?

Reflect
1. Consider a time in your life when you felt that others held you in contempt and were avoiding you. How did it affect you?

What was your relationship with God like during that time? (In particular, how did he encourage you?)

2. David writes that he has "become like broken pottery" (v. 12). At one time or another we have all felt shattered and broken by the events of life. Perhaps you still feel that way (although the events happened a long time ago). Imagine that you are a broken pot. Sit quietly for a while and allow God to put your life back together. After a time of reflection, write down your observations.

Pray
Ask God to help you face graciously whatever difficult circumstances you confront.

Pray for your country, that there would be justice for those who have been deprived of justice by the intrigues of others. Pray for troubled places in the world. Ask God to be a shelter of protection for needy people.

Tell God that you trust him with the "times" of your life. Ask him to make himself known in new ways to you and your family.

DAY 5
Rejoicing in Honor
Psalm 31:19-24

*I*n the conclusion to this psalm David feels a need for honor. He approaches his need in the right way, trusting God to bring public vindication to his leadership in the face of the public humiliation caused by his opponents.

Honor is not a word we use a lot in individualistic Western cultures. Honor implies a public recognition for service to others. We do have words for public recognition today. Words like *fame* and *celebrity* imply personal achievement rather than public contribution. Actors can be famous without being honorable.

The Scriptures strictly forbid us to seek fame and celebrity, but they never exclude the need for honor.

Approach: Settling in God's Presence
A philosopher several centuries ago wrote, "I think, therefore I am." If he were living today he might write, "I am successful, therefore I am."

So much of our sense of self-worth is bound up in setting goals and achieving them. This mindset contributes to our driven and overbusy way of life. If we are going to slow down enough to enjoy the presence of God, we need to escape the idea that our self-worth comes from our achievements. A good way to begin is to turn over all your goals and projects to God. Make a list of everything you want to achieve for the next month or so. In prayer offer the list to God. After you have done that, write down how you feel.

Study

1. Read Psalm 31. How is God's help to David a fitting response to his sense of public humiliation (v. 19)?

2. David's response to God's help is praise. What specific things does David praise God for?

3. David concludes with a couple of admonitions to his readers (vv. 23-24). Write them down, and beside each one write why we should do what he says.

4. Hope in the Lord, verse 24, is another dynamic of waiting on God. Look back through the psalm for ways in which you see David expressing hope.

Reflect

1. We trust God not only for our eternal salvation but also for his help from day to day. As David says, "My times are in your hands" (v. 15). Imagine your life as a play with each day written into the script. Give your script to God, and ask him to be your director and producer. What does it feel like to give up control of your life? Write down your reflections.

What benefits come from having God as your director?

How is waiting involved in having God as your director?

What costs are there?

2. Sometimes God bestows his goodness "in the sight of men." When that happens it is appropriate to feel a sense of honor. Imagine that God has called you up to the front of your church. As he stands beside you, he tells everyone there that he loves you. Write down how that makes you feel.

Pray

Tell God that you are grateful for his goodness. Ask him to work his goodness into your spirit.

Pray that the members of your church would grow in the ability to love the Lord and express their affection for him to each other.

DAY 6

Confession and Forgiveness
Psalm 32:1-5

*J*ust as cholesterol is the silent killer of the physical heart, guilt is the silent killer of our souls. Like cholesterol, guilt collects around the soul and begins to cut off the life-giving supply of God's presence. With cholesterol, there is no single bite that is the fatal killer. It accumulates silently over years, the residue left by a poor diet, inadequate exercise and perhaps genetic malfunction. So it is with guilt. Little by little, with each act of envy, lust, anger, resentment or other sin, guilt accumulates around our spiritual hearts. In advanced states there is a hardening of the heart and a loss of desire for God.

The good news is that God won't let us succumb to the silent killer of guilt without many warnings. He puts his hand on us, creating both inward and outward pain. He increases the pressure until we fall to our knees and call out for help. The exposure of guilt that takes place is not for the purpose of condemnation (as it is for Satan) but in order to cleanse our hearts and restore the flow of his love.

Approach: Settling in God's Presence

A little fear can be a healthy thing. Fear of bad grades can motivate a student to study. Fear of a car accident motivates us to put on our seat belts. But not all fears are healthy. A phobia is a controlling fear that compels us to run and hide even when there is good evidence that we really have nothing to fear. Worry is a less intense form of fear. It gnaws away at us just beneath the surface, below our consciousness. In a subtle but persistent way it distracts us and drains our energy.

If we are to learn to settle in the presence of God, then we need to allow the worries to surface. We also need to name the controlling fears that drive us. Get quiet and ask God to bring to mind your fears in all their varied forms. Write them down and give them over to God. After you have done that, write down any reflections you may have about trusting God.

Study

1. Read Psalm 32 and then focus on verses 1-5. Verses 1 and 2 begin with the word *blessed*. How would you define the word *blessed* from the way David uses it in these verses?

2. In what different ways does David express how God forgives in verses 1 and 2?

3. How is it possible to be a sinner and yet have a spirit without deceit?

4. David had a responsive conscience. How did his unexpressed sin affect him (vv. 3-4)?

5. In what different ways does David describe his confession in verse 5?

Reflect

1. Guilt feelings can cause all kinds of problems. However, they are not necessarily bad. They are good if they move us to repent from sin and to seek forgiveness. But guilt and the resulting repressed feelings can become an inner destructive force that plagues us for years. Perhaps now is the time to search your heart. Consider whether there are things in the past for which you are guilty but have never sought forgiveness. Name those things.

Are there things in the past for which you feel guilty but which were really not wrong? Explain.

2. Several quiet times ago, you imagined your heart as a closet crammed full of clutter. Let's use that image again but change it slightly. Instead of clutter, imagine that it is full of sins that you have chosen not to face. Ask God to open the door of that closet and clean it through the merits of Christ's death on the cross. Sit in quiet and allow God to do his work.

After you have allowed God to do his work, write down your reflections.

Pray

Pray that your family will know the forgiveness of God in Christ.

Ask God to make your church a place where the forgiveness of God in Christ is proclaimed and accepted.

Ask God to make you a messenger of forgiveness to those who have not received God's forgiveness through Christ.

DAY 7
Guidance and Protection
Psalm 32:6-11

There is a debate among Christians as to whether God still actually speaks to us apart from the Bible. A. W. Tozer writes that there are those who believe that for a thousand years or so God was in a speaking mood. During that time, he had people write down what he said. Since that time, if we want to know what God is like we have to go back and read what they wrote. We feel that the Bible is the essential means by which he speaks and the standard by which we recognize his voice. But we find ourselves aligned with those who believe that God's voice is not limited to the Scriptures.

When I believe I hear the Lord speak to me (only once or twice has it been audible), I do not find the experience especially pleasant. It often means I have to change something that I don't want to change. Of course I always find, in the end, that this is a great gift and a means of protection from some action that would hurt me or others.

Approach: Listening to God

In order to cultivate our spiritual ability to hear God, we need to use the "cocked ear" principle. For a while we had a dog named Midnight. In the midst of our noisy house filled with three boys, stereos, TV and sibling competition, he would sit up with his ears pointing straight in the air. Through the din he picked out an unfamiliar noise that he was intensely curious about—for instance, another dog or cat trespassing through our yard.

In the same way, through the constant din of life we can recognize the call of God and his guidance. Imagine that you have spiritual ears. Point them toward heaven today and cultivate an attitude of responsive attention. Sit quietly until you have a sense of being attentive to the voice of God. Write down any observations or impressions you gain from your time of listening.

Study

1. Read Psalm 32. It feels good to be forgiven. How specifically does David respond in verses 6-11?

2. It is interesting that David experienced a sense of protection after receiving forgiveness (v. 7). How might unconfessed sin have made him feel vulnerable and exposed?

3. In verses 8 and 9 David records the Lord's promise of guidance. From these verses, what is the condition of receiving God's guidance?

4. Waiting on the Lord produces humility, responsiveness and trust. How do you see these expressed in this psalm?

Reflect

1. God promises to instruct us and give guidance. Picture yourself before the Lord. Ask him what he wants you to do about the various issues of life facing you. Write down the thoughts and ideas that come to mind. (Keep in mind that Scripture is always the standard by which you evaluate your spiritual perceptions. God doesn't contradict himself and never asks us to do something which he has forbidden in the Scriptures.)

2. One of the reasons that we may not hear the voice of the Lord speaking to us today is that we don't want to. If we know what he is asking us to do, then we are exposed as disobedient if we don't do it. It's much more comfortable to pretend that he doesn't speak or at least that his voice is faint or so obscure as to be confusing. Imagine that you are a fast horse or a strong mule. Allow the Lord to put a bridle on you, and then wait expectantly for the direction that he wants you to go. Write down what it feels like to be responsive to the reins in his hands.

Pray

Ask God to teach you further about how to listen to his voice.

Pray that God's guidance would be made known to the leaders of your church.

DAY 8
Hoping in the Lord's Word
Psalm 33:1-11

*I*n this psalm David meditates on the powerful Word of God by which he creates and sustains his world. Because of the nature of God's Word, we need to open our ears to hear as we read to understand.

After my conversion, I was shocked at what happened when I picked up the Bible. I found myself enticed, confronted, spoken to and challenged. I couldn't get enough of it. Now, almost thirty years later, I still can't get enough. In ways I can't explain, I find through the written Word a personal encounter with God. What I have come to understand is that the words God has spoken are never outdated. Like ripples in a pool that grow as they move out, God's words once spoken continue to move and speak throughout his creation.

Approach: Listening to God
Walk into a classroom of young children without a teacher, and you will

hear lots of noise. Once the children have begun talking, it's difficult to get their attention. However, as any teacher knows, until the children come to order, going on with the lesson is impossible.

In a similar manner, if my own life is in chaos, though I need the Lord's guidance I may not be able to receive it. In order to spend time with God today, stop! Don't try to run your own life; don't tell God what to do. Present your life to God. Ask God to bring in his order. After sitting quietly for a while in expectation of his work, write down your thoughts and feelings.

Study

1. Read Psalm 33. As you can tell by your quiet times so far, Psalms is full of emotions. What is the emotional tone of this psalm?

2. *The word of the Lord* is one of the themes of this psalm. What can you learn about God's Word from verses 1-11?

3. This psalm gives a big picture of God. Other nations thought of their god as a national deity with a limited realm of authority. Over what things does Israel's God have power (vv. 6-11)?

Reflect

1. David writes, "The earth is full of his unfailing love" (v. 5). What a rich image! In contrast to this warm and personal view of the world, today we tend to view the world *merely* as a machine composed of spinning atoms. To get a feel for the biblical perspective, imagine that the sunshine that warms you and the air you breathe are filled with the Lord's love. Sit for a while and soak in his warming love and breathe in his life-sustaining care. After a while, write down your feelings.

2. The psalm begins with a call to sing joyfully. David mentions several ways to use music to celebrate the Word of the Lord. Respond to his call by putting on a worship music tape, taking out a hymnal or writing a verse yourself. However you do it, make music to the Lord.

Pray
Tell God that you need to learn more about his love. Ask him to show you his love through the people around you.

Tell God five things that you appreciate about him.

Ask for God's justice to be worked through the leaders of the nations.

DAY 9

Hoping in the Ruler of the Nations
Psalm 33:12-22

The Nazis wore an iron cross on their uniforms. They were sure that God was on their side. The Ku Klux Klan burns crosses and invokes the Bible to justify racial prejudice. The religious leaders of Jesus' time thought they were on God's side when they sent Jesus to the cross. Such appeals to God for national and public causes are called civil religion. Civil religion is always deficient because it co-opts God for a cause.

Civil religion is essentially an error of previous generations. The new error today is privatism. There is little sense of God's providential control of the nations. Who has any concept of God's involvement in politics, government, business or the course of history? The question we ask of God today is, How can you help me feel better?

This psalm confronts both errors. It reveals a God who uses nations for his purposes while intimately working with individuals. Once we get it right, we see that God is big enough to trust and personal enough to love. However, we will never find that the God of the Bible is available for our personal purposes and causes.

Approach: Listening to the Lord
Ever try talking to someone while you were jogging? It can be done, but phrases come out between puffs and gasps. On the other hand, a nice stroll through the woods or around the block with a friend creates the perfect context for meaningful communication.

If we are going to hear God, then we need to slow down our pace from a dead run or even a steady jog to a casual stroll. Imagine that you are on a walk with God. Or better yet, go for a walk with God. Share with him your feelings, anxieties and concerns. When you come back from your stroll, write down your thoughts and impressions.

Study
1. Read Psalm 33. Israel's God is no mere national god but the One who is over all. According to verses 12-22, what is God's relationship to the world he created?

2. What is his special relationship with "those who fear him" (vv. 18-22)?

3. According to verses 15-18, how are God's special people to think about their own resources and abilities?

4. Describe the experience of waiting mentioned in verses 20-22.

Reflect

1. At one time on the pop charts there was a song about God watching us from a distance. Lots of people liked it, but I didn't. I prefer Jesus' assurance in the Great Commission of Matthew 28:20 that he is with us. However, David does assert in verses 13-14 that God does see us with the perspective that distance provides. Imagine that God watched how you conducted your day from beginning to end. What would he see about your actions?

How do they express your priorities, values and commitments?

Your Actions	Your Priorities, Values, Commitments

2. David says that no army or horse can guarantee success for a king. For one thing, there are always circumstances that are beyond his control. For another, the blessing of God actually determines the outcome of any battle. It is the same for all of life. A stockbroker can't control the stock market. A farmer can't control the weather. Parents can't make their children turn out the way they want them to. How do the limits of your control make learning to wait on God important?

Against this background, consider: What hopes for success do you have that are misdirected? Consider whether you are trusting in your skills, your background, your education, your intelligence, your money, your influence, your friends or other things. After you have identified your false hopes, turn them over to God. Imagine them as idols that you place in his hands. Ask him to take them from you, and then write down what he does with them. Next, make a note about how you feel having turned them loose. (This may be a battle for you. Not everyone can give them over to the Lord the first time they try.)

False Hope	God's Action	Your Feelings

Pray
Ask God to teach you how to work effectively while being dependent on him.

Tell God that you want to learn more about what it means to wait on him.

Pray that rest and hope that come from waiting on the Lord will fill you and your fellow Christians.

DAY 10
Deliverance from Trouble
Psalm 34:1-10

*B*ob's problems seemed overwhelming: trouble in his marriage, trouble at work and trouble with his health. Because I am his pastor, he came to me for help. I wondered what I could say that would make any difference. Even though I knew better, I thought, *God, these problems are too big. What in the world can you do to make a difference?*

At the end of our time together, Bob left with courage and hope. It was not my counseling skills that helped but the psalm you read today, Psalm 34. After we read it, Bob chose to believe that God helps those in desperate situations. None of his problems were fixed when he left, but he knew that he had the help of God. That was enough to go on.

Approach: Listening to God
Winston Churchill once commented, "I love to learn, but I hate to be taught." What is there about us that chafes at putting ourselves under the tutelage of another? It assaults our pride to acknowledge that there are

things we don't know or problems we can't overcome. When we stop trying to do it ourselves, though, we are in a position to receive the help God sends. As you begin your quiet time, make a list of questions you have for God. Don't tell him what to do, just ask. Then sit quietly for a while and listen.

Study

1. Read Psalm 34. How is David feeling toward God? Write down the variety of words that he uses in verses 1-10 to express his current disposition.

2. What benefits are mentioned in verses 1-10 that come to those who seek God's help?

3. What do you think David means by inviting his readers to "taste and see that the LORD is good?"

Reflect

1. David writes of boasting about the Lord. My thesaurus has these words for *boast: brag, crow, gloat* and *vaunt.* It also mentions "strut, swagger or swell." Can you imagine being so proud and grateful to God that you want to brag or crow about him? Has there ever been a time in your life when you felt this way about God? Write down some of the things about God that make you proud.

Choose a fellow believer who won't be put off by your exuberance, and share what you have been feeling.

2. "Taste and see that the LORD is good" (v. 8) is one of my favorite phrases, emphasizing the experiential element of knowing God. The Christian faith includes a pleasurable sensation of the sheer goodness of God. For instance, in Psalm 19 David writes that the Word of God is sweeter than honey. Jesus refers to himself as the bread of life in John 6, and in John 4 as living water. Using these images as a springboard, write a few phrases that draw parallels between some of your favorite tastes and God.

Favorite Tastes	The Character of God

3. How can the goodness of God be a means of strength in the problems that you face?

Pray
Tell God four things that you like about him.

Ask God to increase your ability to "taste and see" that he is with you and that he is good.

Ask God to help you trust him with the pressures of life.

DAY 11
Deliverance for the Needy
Psalm 34:11-22

*D*avid writes this psalm for the spiritually less mature, those who need to be instructed in the ways of God. One thing David thinks we need to know is how to live in a way that brings the blessing of God.

Another essential truth that David thinks we need to know is how to face the hard times. When we hurt, we want to know: Have we done something wrong? Has God deserted us? What do we need to do to receive God's help?

These are good questions. If we pay attention to David in the psalm, we will get some answers.

Approach: Listening to God
I can remember several times my mother had to restrict me during my childhood because I was not *listening* to her. Listening was not a matter of hearing what she said, but of *doing* what she told me to. As you learned

from Psalm 32, God requires us to listen to him in the same way. As you prepare to meet with God today, make a list of your priorities, goals and values. Tell God that you are willing to set aside any of your priorities that don't fit his purposes.

Top Priority for Your Life	Top Priority for This Week

Study

1. Read Psalm 34. Righteousness is a key theme in this psalm. From verses 11-22, write a profile of a righteous person.

2. According to what David writes here, righteousness doesn't guarantee a trouble-free life. What assurances of comfort do the righteous have during times of pain?

3. The opposite of righteousness is wickedness. From verses 16 and 21, what is dangerous about being wicked?

4. God comes to the aid of those who take refuge in him. From this psalm, what does it mean to take refuge in God?

Reflect

1. "Fear of the LORD" is an Old Testament term for respect and submission to God. While it doesn't imply that we should be afraid of God, it does mean being afraid of offending him by conscious disobedience. What temptations are you facing now, and how can learning the fear of the Lord keep you acting and thinking righteously?

Temptations	Acting/Thinking Righteously

2. Those who fear the Lord don't run *from* him but *to* him for refuge (v. 22). As we do, we have the assurance that we won't be condemned. Imagine that you are standing before the Lord in a court scene with accusing circumstances or people. Allow God to be both your judge and your defender. Write down what happens.

After allowing the scene to play out for a while in your imagination, write down the words *not guilty*. That is exactly what God does for all those who place their faith in him through his son Jesus Christ.

Pray

Pray for the young children in your family or extended family. Ask that they know God's love and be responsive to his law. Pray the same thing for the children in your church.

Pray for those you know who are "crushed in spirit." Seek the Lord's comfort and peace for them.

DAY 12
Protection from My Enemies
Psalm 35:1-10

Y ou might be tempted to dismiss this psalm as barbaric and
primitive. It contains angry thoughts of revenge. David calls on
God to "get" those who are trying to hurt him.

But one of the reasons the Psalms are so powerful is that they don't
come from someone with a "managed heart." When David feels hurt,
the anger pours forth in an eloquent torrent.

When hurt, I used to get busy suppressing and restraining all those
negative feelings. I would tell myself, *Christians aren't supposed to feel that
way.* But "managed" emotions lead to "frozen" emotions. If you won't feel
sad, you can't feel happy. If you won't feel angry, you can't feel compas-
sionate.

I have come to believe that Christian maturity is not about reducing
the highs and lows of emotions to a level plane, but about feeling deeply
in a godly way. The issue is not how or what we feel, but what we do
with our emotions. David knows how to take his emotions to God. If we

pay attention to David, we can learn to do that too.

Approach: Listening to God
In our confirmation class this past year I put the students through a Trust Walk. I put blindfolds on some and then teamed each one with a partner who could see. The partner who could see was to guide by means of verbal instruction only (no touching) through an obstacle course that included two sets of stairs and several doors and long hallways. The only way this would work was if the blindfolded person listened to his or her partner *very carefully*.

We can only walk through the obstacles of life if we listen to the voice of the Lord. Get quiet and set your heart to listen to the Lord very carefully so you may receive his clear-sighted direction. Write down any distractions, and hold them up to God for his calming help.

Study
1. Read Psalm 35. This psalm has a militant tone about it. Focus on verses 1-10. What does David mean by the word *salvation,* mentioned in verses 3 and 9, *in the context of these verses*?

2. In your own words describe the different kinds of misfortune David would like to see inflicted on those who have hurt him.

3. What reasons does David give for being so angry?

4. How would waiting on the Lord be a means of protecting David from personal acts of vengeance?

Reflect

1. It is possible to translate the first verse "Attack those who attack me." In the light of Jesus' teaching to "turn the other cheek" and to "pray for those who persecute you," this psalm initially seems contradictory. Yet instead of setting out to inflict pain on his enemies, David expresses his anger to God and asks him to get them back.

Choose one of the times in your life when you were hurt badly. Write out your feelings of pain and anger. After you have written out everything you feel, choose to wait on the Lord for his help.

2. Even as we act graciously toward those who hurt or threaten us, we will still have feelings of hostility and anger. We may not feel gracious toward those who hurt us, but we choose to act that way, not from feelings but from obedience to Jesus Christ. Make a list of those to whom you have felt hostility and anger.

Read Matthew 5:38-48 and ask God to bless those who have hurt you.

Pray

Pray that your church may be characterized by people who know how to be gracious to each other.

Pray for someone you know who does not yet know the grace that God gives through Jesus Christ.

DAY 13

Protection from False Witnesses
Psalm 35:11-18

*A*t one time in my ministry, I worked with a Christian student group that seemed to turn on me. At least that is what it felt like. We had one good year together starting small group Bible studies, planning outreach on campus and conducting a couple of challenging retreats. During that time, I felt a strong sense of partnership with the student leaders.

Toward the middle of the second year, there was a change in tone. My ideas seemed to hit the floor like rocks whenever I made a suggestion. People no longer hung around after meetings to chat with me. Eventually complaints about me began to drift back from a variety of different sources.

I wasn't sure what had happened. What had I done wrong? Who had I offended? I began to question fifteen years of student ministry experience. What was wrong with me? Under such a barrage of internal questioning my leadership became hesitant and tentative. David writes of a similar experience. Instead of allowing his leadership to be immobilized by internalized self-doubt, he turns to God for comfort and help.

Approach: Receiving the Gift of Quiet
When we set our hearts to responsively seek God, there is a strong, settled, quiet rest that can fill our hearts even in the hardest of times. This quiet rest is a gift God gives as we are open to receive it. Ask God to give you his rest as you begin today's quiet time.

Study
1. Read Psalm 35. More reasons for David's anger expressed in the preceding verses are given in 11-18. What do you find out about David's enemies?

2. David laments that he was paid back "evil for good" (v. 12). What good did he do, and what evil did he receive?

3. What does the cry "How long will you look on?" (v. 17) imply about David's sense of God's help?

Reflect
1. Consider a relationship that has gone sour—someone you considered a good friend who, in the end, inflicted pain. Write down the circumstances and how you reacted to them.

2. David writes about his attackers: "Like the ungodly they maliciously mocked." This implies that the attacks came not from the idolatrous but from believers. Certainly down through the ages Christians have turned on each other in anger and then split in hundreds of different denominations. Consider when you have been hurt by fellow Christians. Write down how it affected you and how you responded.

Ask God how he wants you to act toward these believers, and write down your thoughts and impressions as you wait for his answer.

Pray
Thank God for his love for you in the midst of hard times.
    Continue to ask God to bless those with whom you have personal problems.
    Pray for three people in your church.

DAY 14

Protection from Slander
Psalm 35:19-28

Vigilantes, bad leaders and defensive people have something in common. Vigilantes are those who take the law into their own hands. Wicked leaders are those who use the law for their own personal purposes. Defensive people are those who erect emotional barriers to protect themselves.

Vigilantes are dangerous to be around. If they decide you are guilty, then you are subject to their terms of illegal retribution, with no court of appeal. Bad leaders are dangerous to be around because if you get in their way, they will use their power to remove you with no consideration for your personal inconvenience and pain. Defensive people are dangerous to be around because if they think you are a personal threat, you are subject to whatever forces they have at their disposal to protect themselves.

All three, in an illegitimate way, are self-dependent rather than God-dependent. David, during most of his life, turned to God rather than his own resources. For instance, when he had the opportunity to kill Saul during the fugitive years in the desert, he refused to do so. "Shall I kill the Lord's anointed?" was his question. Even as king, when he felt attacked by false friends, he refused to set up a purge. Instead, he poured out his anger to God and asked God for justice.

We may not be rulers, as David is, but we certainly have many occasions to be defensive. The issue is, Will we protect ourselves and perhaps set out for revenge? Or will we call out to God?

Approach: Receiving the Gift of Hunger

Those who know God hunger for him. There is a desire that pulls us from within. As David writes in Psalm 34, we develop a taste for God that only God can satisfy. Before you begin your study, allow a desire for God to rise within you. Write down what you feel.

Study

1. Read Psalm 35. David continues with the description of his adversaries' behavior. What have they done in verses 19-28 to hurt him?

2. How does David want God to defend him from his enemies?

3. The psalm ends with David waiting for his vindication. What benefits does David expect to come from his deliverance?

Reflect

1. David knows that God "delights in the well-being of his servant" (v. 27). I frequently find that people aren't always convinced that God has their well-being in mind, especially when they are struggling with a problem. Unless we are convinced of this, when we enter into times of struggle we will blame God rather than come to him for help. Examine your heart, and write down what you find.

2. When we come through a trying experience with a sense of victory, it is natural to think about what a good job we have done and how cleverly we have faced our problems. David, however, avoids the temptation of personal boasting and gives praise to God. How does waiting on the Lord help us to avoid taking credit that belongs to God?

Think about a recent success that you have experienced and look for as many ways as possible to praise God for it. Write out your expressions of gratitude.

Pray

Pray for the leaders of your church. Ask God to fill them with the assurance of his presence and power.

Thank God for your parents and grandparents. Even if they were less than perfect, they were still a means by which God gave you life and other blessings as well.

DAY 15

Rejection of the Lord's Love
Psalm 36:1-4

The fear of the Lord and the love of the Lord are twin truths that Christians need to have firmly planted in their hearts. God's love could be likened to a carrot on a stick that entices a reluctant pack mule into moving forward. The fear of the Lord is like a stick from behind that prods the mule when it becomes obstinate. We need to be drawn on by the Lord's love, and we need to be prodded by appropriate fear.

If we don't keep both the love of God and the fear of the Lord in mind, then we become unbalanced. The love of the Lord without the fear of the Lord becomes sentimental. The fear of the Lord without his love becomes harsh and oppressive. In this psalm David helps us to see the importance of both.

Approach: Receiving the Gift of God's Presence
While God is present in the world and the heavens declare his glory, we

are inclined by our sin to miss it. I find my vision clears when I begin to write out things I am thankful for. As I write a thank-you for my sons or for the way a meeting went or for the strength I was given to face a problem, I see, in ways that I had missed, that these good things happen because God is with me.

As you prepare to study this psalm, write out your thank-yous to the Lord and look for his presence in your life.

Study

1. Read Psalm 36. Focus on verses 1-4. David reflects on the character of the wicked. Describe the character of a wicked person from verses 1-4.

2. Describe the dynamics of a wicked person's relationship to God.

3. What decisions does a wicked person make that lead to a sinful life?

4. What delusions does a wicked person have that contribute to living a sinful life?

Reflect

1. While we may not fit the description of the wicked, we all have the potential to choose the way of sin. We do well to search our own hearts in light of God's Word. David writes that flattery and self-conceit create a blindness to God and to our own sinfulness. Imagine yourself standing before God. Ask him to remove any blinders you have put over your spiritual eyes, and then wait quietly to see what he does. After some time in reflection, write down what happened.

2. From time to time we all have sinful thoughts that pass through our minds. The wicked, however, do not reject such thoughts. Instead, they choose to entertain them and then make a commitment to act upon them. Write down some thoughts you have chosen to reject recently because you knew they were wrong.

After you have done that, give thanks to God that he has been so active in helping you choose what is right. If you find that you have let some ungodly ideas settle in your heart, reject them now and ask God to cleanse and redirect your thinking patterns.

Pray
Pray for the godly character of friends and family members. Ask God to give them the strength to reject ungodly thoughts.
Pray that you too will have the strength to reject ungodly thoughts.
Pray for the godly character of Christian leaders. Ask God to give them the strength to reject ungodly thoughts.

Day 16
The Fountain of the Lord's Love
Psalm 36:5-12

My need for love is embarrassing. When I acknowledge that I need love, it means that I am not complete in myself. To receive love, I must look to someone else. To make matters worse, I find that my need for love is inexhaustible. Yesterday's love is not enough for today.

Our need for love means we need people—friends, spouses, family members. Yet even if all those people loved us perfectly, we still wouldn't have enough love to meet our need. David celebrates the good news that God's supply of love is more than sufficient. God's love reaches to the heavens and has more substance than the biggest mountains.

If we are convinced of the abundance of God's love, then we can be open to admitting our need, and we can be free to share it with others.

Approach: Receiving the Gift of Love
When I was in college the Beatles were singing, "All you need is love."

(That dates me.) I agree. We all need love. However, I have found that needing love and receiving love are two different things. Because of pains of the past, pride, blindness or many other reasons, people who need it most often can't take it in. Like water raining on parched soil and running off, love may run off a hurting heart.

Consider how open you are to receiving love from God, your family, friends and fellow Christians. Ask God to soften your heart as you prepare to spend time in his Word. Sit quietly. Give over to God any hardening factors that you can discern.

Study

1. Read Psalm 36. David observes that there is no fear of the Lord before the eyes of the wicked. From verses 5-9, what is it that they are blind to?

2. Initially, David seems to jump without transition from musing on the wicked to writing on the love of God. However, in verses 10-12 he ties the two themes together. What do these verses tell you about David's experiences?

3. We learn a great deal about the specific love of God in these verses. What important truth can you know about God from verse 12?

4. What in this passage would encourage you to wait for God's love?

Reflect

1. David writes that the Lord's love reaches to the heavens and extends to every corner of his creation. However, for lots of reasons it's hard to believe that the Lord loves us. Consider your own ability to accept the Lord's love and his benefits. What hesitations do you have that the Lord loves you?

How do your hesitations manifest themselves?

What would have to happen for you to be more open to his love?

2. The Spanish explorer Hernando de Soto spent years wandering around Florida looking for the fountain of youth. He never found it because it doesn't exist. However, the fountain of life does. It flows from the heart of God, and all who want may drink of it. Imagine that you are splashing in this fountain. Drink from it and allow it to wash over you. Allow it to refresh you, quench your thirst and cleanse you from sin. After enjoying the fountain of God's life, write down how you have been nourished by it.

Pray

Pray that the members of your church would have the ability to accept the Lord's love.

Pray that God would make his love overflow in you so that you could share it with others.

DAY 17
The Safety of the Land
Psalm 37:1-7

*T*he theme song to the Broadway hit *West Side Story* includes the line, "There's a place for us, somewhere a place for us." The song is the heart's cry of young lovers frustrated by racial prejudice. As they face the impossibility of their love, they long for someplace other than the gang-controlled war zone of West Side New York City.

A place to belong is a continuing object of human longing and conflict. The Promised Land—its acquisition, loss and repossession—is one of the central themes of the Old Testament. Today that same land is the constant cause of conflict between the Palestinians and Jews. And wars in Europe, Asia, Africa and throughout the world are driven by the desire to have a piece of land to call home.

In this psalm David describes how God's people can receive and inhabit the safe place he has for all who trust in him.

Approach: Receiving the Gift of Guidance

God hasn't left us to figure out life on our own. We have an inclination, however, to be the captains of our fates. We want to be in charge of our own lives if at all possible. Consider: if God came to you with a specific set of instructions on how to face your pressing issues, and if those instructions went directly against how you wanted to handle things, how would you respond?

As you prepare for your time with God today, ask him to open your heart to receive his guidance for you.

Study

1. Read Psalm 37. David gives an unusually extensive list of exhortations to his readers in verses 1-7. Write them out in your own words.

2. What benefits does God give to those who live this way?

3. We are not to worry when those who are evil succeed (v. 6). Why not?

4. How will meditating on these verses allow us to enjoy safe pastures?

Reflect

1. David encourages us to enjoy safe pasture in the land. This is one of

my favorite images. Enter into it by imagining that you are in a green field surrounded by woods and a stream. Perhaps you might want to put a small cabin in the field or by the stream. Put a porch on the cabin and a couple of rocking chairs on it, one for you and one for the Lord. Now sit with the Lord, look out at the beauty around you and just enjoy being in his presence. After a while, make some notes on how this exercise affected you.

2. David encourages you to "delight yourself in the LORD." What do you find delightful about knowing God?

What hesitations or inhibitions do you have that would keep you from delighting in God?

3. What have you found delightful about your life in the past year or two?

4. What do you find delightful about knowing God?

Pray
Ask God to teach you how to delight in him.

Pray for the homeless, that God would give them himself and give them a place to rest.

DAY 18

Peace in the Land
Psalm 37:8-17

Coming to a narrow spot in the road during a Sunday afternoon ride, I got off and walked my bike. I'd gone only a short distance when a car swerved toward me rather than away. I dove for the ditch. As the car drove off, I was filled with indignation and rage. What the driver did was foolish, but I was surprised at the intensity of my fuming response. I wanted to yell and shake my fist. I made a mental note that something was out of place in my spirit. In my quiet time a couple of days later I discovered a list of unresolved hurts and growing grudges. I set aside my Bible reading for the day and had a time of heart-cleaning with the Lord.

David says that for us to enjoy peace in the land we have to "refrain from anger and turn from wrath." Angry hearts and indignant people, even when the cause is just, can increase conflict and obstruct possible solutions. Families, offices and churches become places of tension when there is "righteous" indignation. Angry people find all kinds of new reasons to be angry. Frequently, their angry eruptions contain rage from the past and the present. This is not the way of peace.

While David calls us to refrain from anger, he is not calling us to deny it. We have seen that David experienced his share of anger. But he is calling us to deal with our anger in a godly way. If you pay attention to what he says, then you will find a new way of coping with anger. In doing so, you will find peace in your heart and will also bring peace to those around you.

Approach: Receiving the Gift of Peace

On occasion sharp disagreements arise between our three boys that erupt into shouting matches. The first step in resolving a problem is getting everyone to stop shouting.

God wants us to have peace in the conflicts we face. The first step to receiving his peace is to stop shouting so loudly. (If we aren't actually shouting out loud, we are usually doing so in our hearts.) Once we stop, he can sort things out. Put down the burdens and fights you face. Give them to God, and allow him to speak peace to your heart. Write down any insights you gain.

Study

1. Read Psalm 37. This psalm develops the contrasts between the wicked and the righteous. In order to put the differences in perspective, fill out the two lists below for verses 8-17.

The Wicked	The Righteous

2. How are God's people treated by the wicked?

3. How does God respond to the wicked?

4. What do you think a believer's attitude should be toward the wicked?

5. Against the backdrop of the wicked, how is God's promise of peace and land an encouragement?

Reflect

1. We are exhorted to refrain from anger and to turn from wrath because it leads to evil. Think of a time when anger has gotten you into trouble. Why were you angry, and how did it affect you and those around you?

How might waiting on the Lord help you deal with your feelings of anger, even if the anger is an inappropriate emotional response on your part?

2. Jesus echoes this psalm in the Beatitudes when he teaches, "Blessed are the meek, for they will inherit the earth" (Matthew 5:5). We tend to think of meek people negatively, as pushovers. Considering today's verses, how might meekness actually be a display of superior strength and knowledge?

How would meekness alter your behavior around your home, your work and your church?

Pray
Pray for those who are angry at you. Ask God to bless them.
   Pray that meekness would characterize the members of your church.

DAY 19

The Inheritance of the Land
Psalm 37:18-24

When we think about life, our emphasis comes down on what we must do. "God helps those who help themselves," you know. "Success comes to those who set a goal and work hard." "Those who are effective achieve the greatest amount in the least amount of time." These stock phrases characterize the ways we think.

In contrast, receiving an inheritance from God puts the emphasis on him. We can work for success, but we can only wait for an inheritance. Actually, there is something else we can do—make sure that we are on good terms with the relative who is willing it to us. Instead of effectiveness and productivity the essential values become faithfulness, integrity and trustworthiness. And we still don't earn what we inherit. It comes to us as a gift, an expression from someone who loves us.

Approach: Settling Through Praise
When we take our minds off ourselves and put them on God, our world

is put into order. Spend time praising God for his ability to know you and the details of your life while continuing to manage the swirling galaxies. Write down as many good things as you can about God's ability to know you and his universe.

Study

1. Read Psalm 37. What are the contrasts between the blameless and the wicked in verses 18-24?

The Wicked	The Righteous (Blameless)

2. What can we know about the future of the wicked?

3. How is God active in the lives of people in these verses?

4. What are the benefits that come to the righteous in the end?

5. What role does waiting have in receiving and inheritance?

Reflect

1. David emphasizes the theme of inheritance in these verses. How can

the anticipation of a future inheritance affect the way we live today in our relationships?

our use of money?

our possessions?

2. Let's get more specific. If you knew that all you could want is coming to you in five years, how would it affect your actions and decisions today?

3. David writes that in times of disaster the righteous will have plenty. Have you experienced a time of hardship when you were sustained by the Lord? Write down ways the Lord met your needs.

How was waiting involved in receiving the Lord's help?

Pray
Pray for those you know who are facing hard times. Ask God to bring his comfort, protection and provision.
   Ask God to turn the hearts of the "wicked" to repentance and faith in Jesus Christ.

DAY 20
The Reward of the Land
Psalm 37:25-36

*A*s a new Christian, I was sure that life would be easier than it had been. My salvation was noteworthy to myself and my friends. I had been in deep trouble, emotionally, spiritually and academically. My salvation brought visible, revolutionary changes to all those areas. Everyone knew that *something* had happened to Steve.

Looking back several decades, I know the changes were real. But I'm not so quick to say that becoming a Christian makes life easier. I have found both Christian ministry and the Christian life to be hard. We all face a "long obedience in the same direction." What needs to be affirmed is that while the Christian life is not necessarily easy, it is worth it.

This psalm is written from the long-term view of knowing God. David looks back over nearly eighty years. He affirms that God keeps his promises and brings rewards to those who trust him. He knows from experience what he is talking about.

Approach: Settling Through Praise and Thanksgiving
Consider the staggering fact that the Creator of time and eternity loves you. Write down ten things you can think of about the love of God.

Study
1. Read Psalm 37. From verses 25-36, describe the character and actions of the righteous.

2. Describe the relationship between the wicked and the righteous in verses 32-36.

3. What resources do we have to handle the enmity of the wicked?

4. From David's observations, what does God require of the righteous in order to reward them with the gift of the land?

Reflect
1. David writes of the benefits of trusting the Lord from his perspective as a old man. How long have you been in a living relationship with God?

What benefits have you received?

2. Waiting on the Lord implies that certain things are beyond our control, or at least are better left in his hands even if we could take charge. Finding the balance between working and waiting is not easy. Make a list of things that you want most in life over the next ten years. Place the list in his hands and sit for a while in quiet. Tell God you will be faithful in your efforts but will look to him to bring these things about in his timing and wisdom.

After taking such a long-term view, focus on the issues that you face this week. Write down your tasks and tell God that you are willing to both work and wait on each of these issues.

Pray
Ask God to bring spiritual and numerical growth to his church around the world and to your church.

Ask God to bless those who have been faithful and godly believers for the duration of their lives. Ask that the power of their godly lives would spread to the younger members of your congregation.

DAY 21

The Honor of the Lord
Psalm 37:37-40

W ant to know how to succeed? The contemporary success
formula is *Effort + Method = Success*. Work hard with the right
technique and you are sure to make it big. Failure to achieve
success is easy to diagnose. Either you haven't worked hard enough or
you don't have the right method.

David's prescription for success is different from the contemporary
one. His formula is *Don't sin. When you get into trouble, seek God's help.*
What David's approach includes that the contemporary one doesn't is
the knowledge that we live in a supernatural world that has a moral
foundation. The contemporary formula ignores the action of a divine
being who can bless or thwart your efforts. It also misses the moral
behavior that the divine ruler requires. No matter what you achieve in the
short run, it is a fact of reality that God doesn't like sin and therefore "sinners
will be destroyed." Under these conditions, present success for those who
sin will mean ultimate failure. As we think about the future, we would be

wise to take David's simple but profound advice very seriously.

Approach: Settling Through Praise and Thanksgiving

Jesus saves! An eternal mystery and glorious truth. In some circles, perhaps, a truth trivialized through empty repetition. As you are discovering through these psalms, God's salvation is rich, encompassing and practical. Write down seven good things about a God who helps and delivers his people in times of trouble.

Study

1. Read Psalm 37. David invites us to join him in his concluding reflections in verses 37-40 on the outcome of a righteous life. Look over the entire psalm and summarize the reasons given for choosing God's way rather than the way of the wicked.

Give you own reasons for choosing the way of righteousness.

2. In what ways does David describe the relationship between God and the righteous in verses 37-40?

3. In the end, no matter how things appear at present, the righteous will triumph. How does that affect your thoughts and feelings?

Reflect

1. Those who walk with God have a constant stronghold on which they can lean for stability. Picture yourself being able to stand against the strong winds of life because you are being held firmly by the Lord. Write down what difference that will make in the way you think and act today.

2. David urges us to consider the blameless and to observe the upright. Think of people you know who have walked in faith for a lifetime. What are they like?

What is there about them that inspires you?

Pray

David is clear: "The wicked will be cut off." Pray that the good news of Jesus Christ would spread throughout your community and our world so that people may receive the righteousness of God.

Pray for someone you know who needs a relationship with Jesus Christ.

DAY 22
Rebuke and Judgment
Psalm 38:1-8

*I*n this psalm David describes a time of pain which he attributes in great measure to his sin and the resulting judgment of God.

Hold it! Red flags fly!

Once we admit this, I see all kinds of opportunities for abuse. All we need are a few friends like the ones Job had. Armed with this doctrine of the judgment of God, they will be eager to tell us when we are hurting, "This hard thing happened to you because you have sinned. Repent. God is judging you." Actually, I don't need Job's friends to abuse such an idea. As soon as something difficult arises I wonder, "What have I done wrong? Is God judging me?"

As I read David's words, despite the danger for abuse I must ask, "Does God really cause pain because of something I have done wrong?" From this psalm, Psalm 30, Hebrews 12:4-11 and other Scriptures, I must conclude that he does.

Initially this is not a happy thought. However, if I am willing to acknowledge that God blesses me, I must be willing to acknowledge that he disciplines me as well. As the author of Hebrews writes, "The Lord disciplines those he loves." Hard things may be sent as discipline to convey that God has not left me alone in my folly. He refuses to let me go my own way. This is good news indeed!

While I affirm that my experiences may convey the blessing or the judgment of God, I must be careful. I don't understand all that the Lord does. What appears to be a blessing may not be, while what appears to be judgment may not be either.

A little light from David may help with this difficult issue.

Approach: Settling Through Praise and Thanksgiving

"Condemned to freedom" was one existentialist philosopher's description of a world without a God. In the same vein, Charles Manson, the mass murderer, is reputed to have said, "If God is dead, what is wrong?"

The good news is that God is not dead. It is also good that he places restraints on us and disciplines us for our benefit. We need to thank God that he loves us enough to actively restrain our inclinations to temptation and sin. Praise God for as many of the Ten Commandments as you can remember. As you write out your praise, include any other commandments you can think of.

Study

1. Read Psalm 38. David writes during a time of great pain. What images does he use in verses 1-8 to describe his situation?

2. What reasons can you discover for his all-encompassing pain in these verses?

3. How would you assess David's attitude toward his physical and spiritual condition?

4. Describe David's attitude toward God in the midst of his afflictions.

5. How was David waiting in the wrong way?

Reflect
1. We tend to see our emotional and physical health as the result of circumstances, germs and body chemistry. When we are feeling badly, we suspect a breakdown in one or more of those areas. David attributes his ill-health, in this psalm, to his own sin and the discipline of God. We would do well to take David seriously. But we need to be careful too. What dangers and what benefits come from thinking of our physical, emotional and spiritual states as the result of the discipline of God?

Dangers	Benefits

2. Although we think it is worth asking, we include this next question with caution, as we all see spiritual truth through a dark glass, and our insights are never completely clear this side of heaven. What blessings and what discipline do you think you have received from the Lord over the past year or so?

Blessings	Discipline

Respond to the Lord by thanking him for his blessings.

Repent and seek forgiveness for sins that he has exposed. Whatever you do, don't condemn yourself. God doesn't. He is always quick to extend his grace. Be as quick to receive it.

Pray
Pray for those who are hurting. Ask God to give them strength, encouragement and comfort.

Pray that those who are in pain may be shaped and molded by their experience into a deeper walk with God and godly Christian character.

DAY 23

Confession and Hope
Psalm 38:9-22

Recently, I received a difficult phone call from one of my committee leaders. I'd started a new program that several people were not pleased about. They were complaining not only about the program but also about the way the decision was made. As I listened to the objections from the head of the committee, I was forced to admit they had a point. My ideas may have been good, but I cut out several people in the implementation process, and they had a right to be upset.

David shows the kind of response God wants. In the midst of a defensive position, he can face up to his own failures. "I confess my iniquity," he says, "I am troubled by my sin."

Healthy Christian relationships are not easy, but they are possible. When we avoid the "I'm right no matter what" syndrome, the way is open for real Christian community.

Approach: Settling Praise and Thanksgiving
God is constantly rescuing us from tight spots. Some of those tight spots
we are aware of, most we are not. Write out a list of thank-yous to God
for as many instances of his help as you can think of.

Study
1. Read Psalm 38. What physical, social and spiritual afflictions is David
experiencing in verses 9-22?

Physical	Social	Spiritual

2. How does David approach God to get help?

3. What specific things does David want God to do to help him with his
pain?

4. What do you learn in these verses about prayer and waiting?

Reflect
1. David is in a doubly painful situation. Although he is experiencing

rejection and persecution, he acknowledges that he has sinned and shares in the responsibility for his affliction. When have you experienced pain that was at least partly your fault?

How did you handle it?

What was painful about the experience?

What can you learn from David's example?

2. The theme of waiting comes up again, as it does throughout the Psalms. Here David's waiting, according to verses 21 and 22, has an urgency about it. In your imagination, put yourself in a place where you are dependent on God and need him to act in a hurry. Write down any insights you gain about yourself and God.

Pray
Pray for those whom you have offended this past year. Ask God's blessing on them.
   Pray for family members whom you have hurt or alienated. Ask God to bring reconciliation.

DAY 24
Facing Life's End
Psalm 39:1-6

Jane Walmsley, television correspondent and commentator on American life, says, "Americans think that death is optional: They may not admit it, and will probably laugh if it's suggested; but there is a nagging suspicion that you can delay death (or who knows, avoid it altogether) if you really try. This explains the common pre-occupation with health, aerobics, prune-juice, plastic surgery and education" (*Brit-think, Ameri-think*, p. 9).

That hope of eluding death flies in the face of reality. No one has done it. Life this side of the Fall is 100 percent fatal. David would say that only those who have faced their death can really live life properly. In this psalm he asks God to help him take a long-term view of life, and as you shall read, that includes the impending prospect of death.

Approach: Settling Through Thanksgiving and Praise
When he was little, one of our sons asked, "Where does God come from

and when was he born?" Our response was as amazing to him as it continues to be to us: "God always has been." While we can never quite get our minds around this, the good news is that an eternal God can offer eternal life. Write out expressions of praise and thanksgiving for benefits of our immortal God.

Study
1. Read Psalm 39. Remembering that the Psalms combine life experience, knowledge of God and emotions, how would you describe David's mood and situation in this psalm?

2. David chooses to be silent in the presence of some hostile people. What effect does David's silence have on him in verses 1-6?

3. When David breaks his silence, he does so by offering a prayer to face his mortality. What does David know (vv. 5-6), and what does he want to know (v. 4)?

Reflect
1. Following David's example, ask God to help you see as much about your own mortality as you can handle. Sit quietly waiting for the Lord's insight. Write down what benefits you can perceive from facing your own death.

2. How does considering your own motality affect the way you think of the present and the future?

the way you think about your possessions?

the way you think about your relationships?

3. How does the knowledge of eternal life through Jesus Christ affect your reflections?

4. What does facing your own mortality teach you about waiting on the Lord?

Pray

Pray for those you know who are sick. Ask God to give them the courage to face life and death.

Pray that many who are ill will hear the good news of eternal life through faith in Jesus Christ.

DAY 25

Facing God's Judgment
Psalm 39:7-13

*T*here was a time when Jackie and I felt the judgment of God. I mishandled some money. Although it was not immoral or illegal, I used the money in a way contrary to what I knew God was calling me to do. As we talked over the consequences, Jackie and I saw them as a discipline. However, during that time of discipline, we experienced the tremendous affirmation, love and blessing of God. Instead of feeling rejected and deserted, we felt his overwhelming presence.

God is both just and merciful. If he were merciful without justice, his laws and moral governance of our lives would be meaningless. (Countries collapse into chaos without the rule of law.) But if God were not merciful, an execution of his justice would doom all of us to exile in a Christless eternity. God's justice means we are accountable for our actions, but that because of his mercy we aren't doomed by them.

In this psalm David reflects these twin themes. He wants to run from God's presence because of the pain his sin creates. On the other hand, he runs to God as his only means of hope.

Approach: Settling Through Detachment
The first commandment, "You shall have no other gods before me," and Jesus' call, "Follow me," require us to place everything second in priority behind our Lord. Think about everything you own. Write down your most valued possessions one by one and give them over to the Lord. When you are done, sit in a quiet trust that comes from surrender to him.

Study
1. Read Psalm 39. This a psalm of judgment. In your own words, describe God's approach toward sin in verses 7-13.

2. What does David desire from God?

3. David laments that he feels like a stranger. What is causing him to feel that way?

4. David uses the word *look* in verses 7 and 13. What seemingly contradictory things is he asking for?

How can you reconcile them?

Reflect

1. Abraham and his sons were merely sojourners in Palestine. Although David is now king of the land that had been given by God, he is feeling like a stranger and an alien. Consider times when you felt like you didn't belong. What causes such a sense of strangeness?

How did your sense of alienation affect your relationship with God?

2. David appeals for God to save him from his transgressions. A thousand years later, through the work of Jesus Christ on the cross, God dealt once for all with the problem of sin. Make a list of your sins and see yourself placing them at the foot of the cross.

What difference will this make in the way you think and live today?

Pray

Ask God to bring help to refugees who have been displaced by famine or war.

Pray that the ministry of your church will offer the grace of Jesus Christ to those who feel the weight of their sin.

Pray that God will show you what it means to find a home in his love.

DAY 26
A *Celebration of Waiting*
Psalm 40:1-10

*P*salm 40 is the last psalm in this series of guided quiet times. You have been with David and us through some ups and downs of life and have faced some of the emotions in the depth of the human heart. We hope you are learning that waiting on the Lord is a way of life—a mental, emotional and volitional disposition.

Psalm 40 is a fitting termination to our times together, because here David brings together many of the themes implicit in a life of waiting. In this psalm you will find a radical reordering of relationships, worship, security and spiritual desire. Most of all, you will be reminded that you are not alone. God is there and delights to come to the aid of those who trust him. If the struggles that you faced at the beginning of your study in this guide are not yet resolved, take heart. It is good for you to learn to wait. Through your waiting and perhaps hurting, God is working in you and for you. He will come through for you. If you have experienced his deliverance through this time of study, be sure to note and share in

David's celebration of God's help.

Approach: Settling Through Detachment
Today, consider your primary relationships in light of the first commandment and Jesus' call to discipleship. Give over each person to his care, and place them second in your life behind your allegiance to him. Make written observations about how this exercise affected you.

Study
1. Read Psalm 40. In verse 2 David rejoices in God's deliverance from a "slimy pit" to a "firm place." What do you think he means by that?

2. In response to God's help, David proclaims righteousness, doesn't seal his lips, doesn't hide God's righteousness, and does not conceal God's love. From your reading of verses 1-10, what is he eager to make known?

3. The normal response of gratitude was to make an offering. How is David's response different?

4. Consider David's public proclamation in this psalm in contrast with his silence in the preceding one. What role does public testimony have in spiritual health?

Reflect
1. Waiting in a slimy pit—what a graphic picture of needing God's help! Imagine that you are in a slimy pit from which you need deliverance. What things in your life have placed you in that pit, and what makes it "slimy"?

As you call out for God to deliver you, what is it like to wait on God?

2. Celebration and public testimony are the appropriate responses to being delivered from a pit to a firm place. Write down several things that you could say to a friend about how good God is to you.

Once you have done that, make plans to share with several people, in an appropriate and casual way, the things that you have written.

Pray
Thank God for as many things about him that you can think of.

Ask God to give you a heart of dependence and gratitude.

Pray that others in your church would enter into new celebration of the goodness of God.

DAY 27
Learning to Wait on the Lord
Psalm 40:11-17

*J*udy had a portable phone beside her; she was about to become a grandmother for the first time. During the entire Bible study, Judy contributed to our discussion. However, if that phone had rung with news of her daughter-in-law's labor, Judy would have been out of there in a minute.

Those who have faith in Jesus Christ are born again by the Spirit. Yet we are still in the process of being born—groaning with birth pangs as we wait for the completion of our adoption as children of God (Romans 8:23). There is a day coming when Jesus Christ will come back and consummate his redemptive work. When that happens there will be no more pain, sorrow, tears or suffering. All our waiting for immediate needs is a small part of the real wait, which is for Jesus Christ to come. Jesus Christ wants us to wait for him, living on tiptoe. Maranatha!

Approach: Settling Through Detachment
You have done exercises to detach youself from possessions and rela-

tionships. Now it is appropriate to detach from yourself as well. Jesus calls his disciples to deny themselves, take up their cross and follow him. Commit yourself body and soul to him. As reservations or objections rise to the surface, write them down. Give those to him and ask him to take them from you.

Study

1. Read Psalm 40. Compare verses 1-10 with verses 11-17. How does the psalm's tone change in the second half?

2. Considering the attitude of David in these verses, put into your own words David's description of life's dilemma.

What effect does it have on him?

3. In Scripture God refers to David as "a man after his own heart." In this psalm we get a unique glimpse of David's character. From this psalm, describe David in his relationship to God.

4. David begins this psalm by saying he waited patiently. He concludes by asking that God would not delay. What do the elements of patience and the need for a speedy answer contribute to your understanding of what it means to wait on God?

Reflect
1. David is threatened by others who oppose him and by his own sins. We saw this theme in Psalm 38. How are these twin themes a continuing presence in your own life?

2. Evidently relational struggles and sin are things even a mature believer has to deal with throughout life. How can the principle of waiting on God be a continuing source of strength and comfort in this struggle?

3. Imagine that you knew for certain that Jesus Christ was coming back in one week. How would you spend your week waiting?

How can you apply this experience of waiting to the duration of time until he returns?

Pray
Ask Jesus Christ to come back soon.
    Pray for your loved ones who don't yet have a relationship with Jesus Christ. Ask the Spirit to give them hungry hearts for his love.
    Pray that your church would be characterized by those who live in a waiting anticipation for the return of Jesus Christ.